ROGER BERLIND   ROGER HORCHOW   DARYL ROTH
JANE BERGERE   TED HARTLEY   CENTER THEATRE GROUP
present
DAVID HYDE PIERCE *and* DEBRA MONK
in
CURTAINS

Book by	*Music by*	*Lyrics by*
RUPERT HOLMES	JOHN KANDER	FRED EBB

Original Book and Concept by	*Additional Lyrics by*
PETER STONE	JOHN KANDER *and* RUPERT HOLMES

Starring

KAREN ZIEMBA

JASON DANIELEY   JILL PAICE
and
EDWARD HIBBERT

Also Starring

JOHN BOLTON   MICHAEL X. MARTIN   MICHAEL McCORMICK
NOAH RACEY   ERNIE SABELLA   MEGAN SIKORA

with

ASHLEY AMBER   NILI BASSMAN   KEVIN BERNARD   WARD BILLEISEN   PAULA LEGGETT CHASE   JENNIFER DUNNE
DAVID EGGERS   J. AUSTIN EYER   MATT FARNSWORTH   PATTY GOBLE   MARY ANN LAMB   BRITTANY MARCIN
JIM NEWMAN   JOE AARON REID   DARCIE ROBERTS   CHRISTOPHER SPAULDING   ALLISON SPRATT   JEROME VIVONA

Set Design	*Costume Design*	*Lighting Design*
ANNA LOUIZOS	WILLIAM IVEY LONG	PETER KACZOROWSKI

Sound Design	*Hair and Wig Design*	*Dance Arrangements*
BRIAN RONAN	PAUL HUNTLEY	DAVID CHASE

Fight Direction	*Aerial Effects Design*	*Make-Up Design*	*Associate Choreographer*
RICK SORDELET	PAUL RUBIN	ANGELINA AVALLONE	JOANN M. HUNTER

Casting	*Production Supervisor*	*Technical Supervisor*	*Music Coordinator*
JIM CARNAHAN, CSA	BEVERLEY RANDOLPH	PETER FULBRIGHT	JOHN MONACO

General Management	*Marketing Services*	*Press Representative*	*Associate Producers*
101 PRODUCTIONS, LTD.	TMG- THE MARKETING GROUP	BONEAU/BRYAN-BROWN	BARBARA AND PETER FODOR

Orchestrations
WILLIAM DAVID BROHN

Music Director/Vocal Arrangements
DAVID LOUD

Choreography by
ROB ASHFORD

Directed by
SCOTT ELLIS

AMERICAN PREMIERE PRODUCED AT THE AHMANSON THEATRE BY CENTER THEATRE GROUP, LA'S THEATRE COMPANY

Production photos © Joan Marcus

ISBN 978-1-4234-4739-9

HAL•LEONARD®
CORPORATION
7777 W. BLUEMOUND RD. P.O. BOX 13819 MILWAUKEE, WI 53213

Visit Hal Leonard Online at
www.halleonard.com

David Hyde Pierce

Jill Paice and David Hyde Pierce

Jason Danieley

Karen Ziemba

Karen Ziemba, Noah Racey and Company

Karen Ziemba, Debra Monk, David Hyde Pierce, Michael McCormick and Edward Hibbert

Jill Paice, David Hyde Pierce and Company

Ensemble

(l-r) Christopher Spaulding, Ward Billeisen, Michael X. Martin, Debra Monk, Michael McCormick, Kevin Bernard and Joe Aaron Reid

Company

Jill Paice, David Hyde Pierce and Company

Ensemble

(l-r) Christopher Spaulding, Ward Billeisen, Michael X. Martin, Debra Monk,
Michael McCormick, Kevin Bernard and Joe Aaron Reid

Company

WIDE OPEN SPACES

Music and Lyrics by
JOHN KANDER

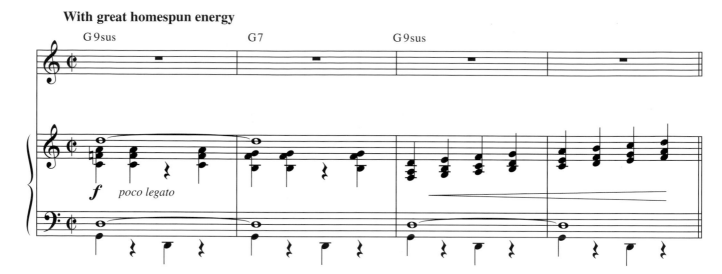

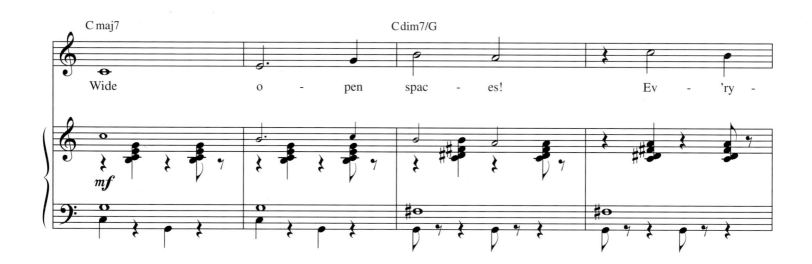

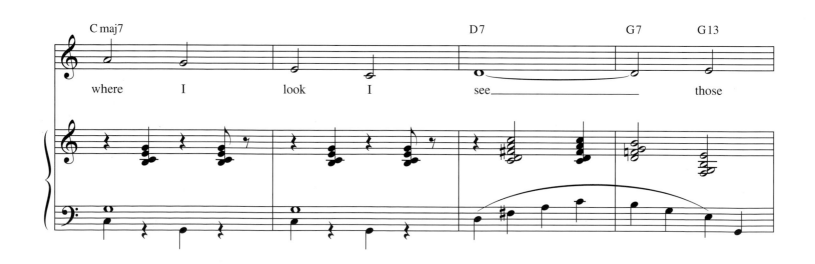

WHAT KIND OF MAN

Music by JOHN KANDER
Lyrics by FRED EBB

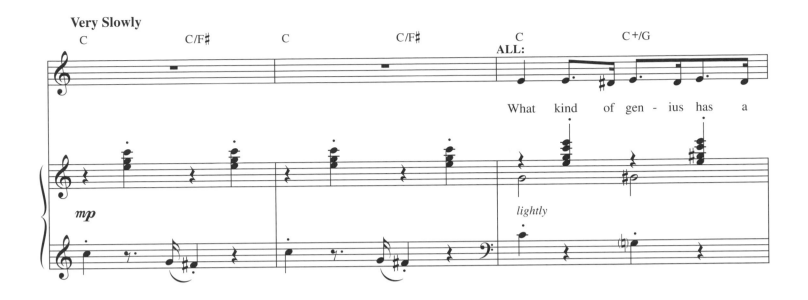

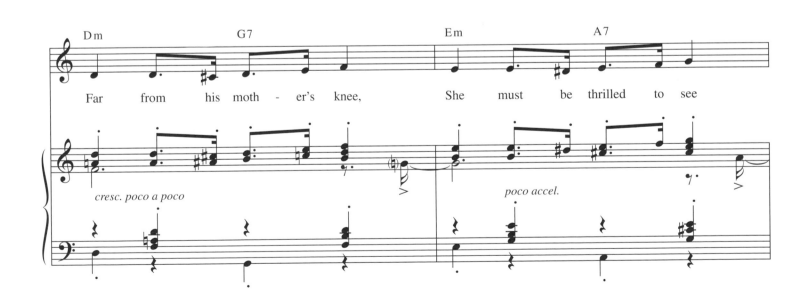

THINKING OF HIM

Music by JOHN KANDER
Lyrics by FRED EBB

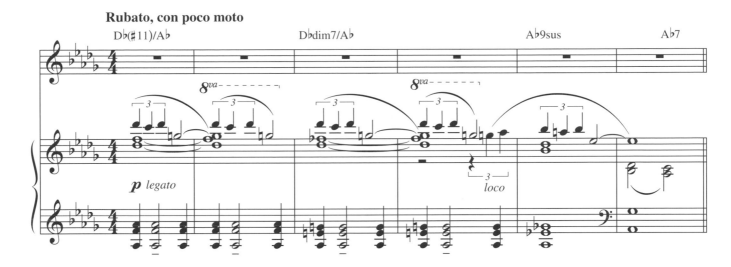

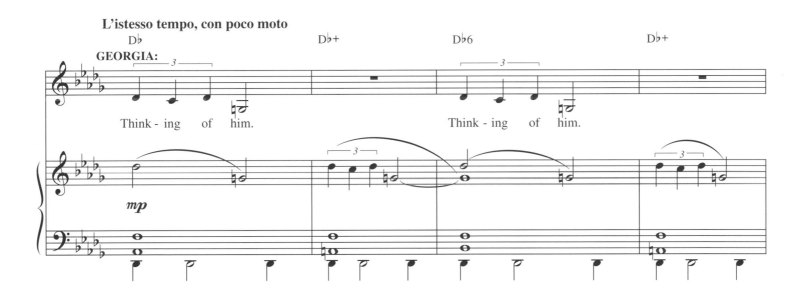

GEORGIA:

Think - ing of him. Think - ing of him.

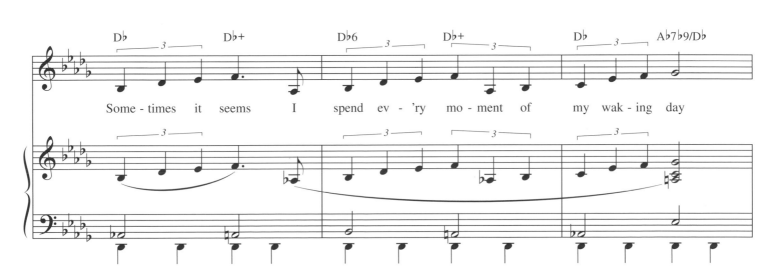

Some - times it seems I spend ev - 'ry mo - ment of my wak - ing day

TOWN WITHOUT PITY

from the 1961 Motion Picture *TOWN WITHOUT PITY*

Words and Music by DIMITRI TIOMKIN
and NED WASHINGTON

Gently, flowing

When you're young and so in love as we, and be-

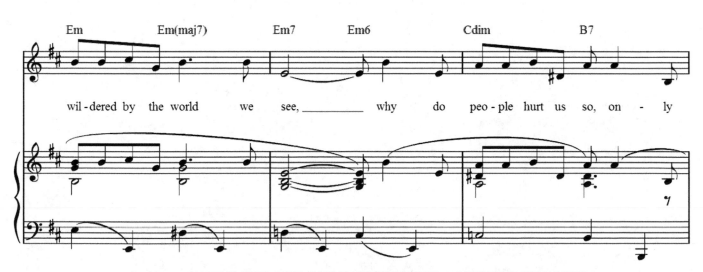

wil-dered by the world we see,_____ why do peo-ple hurt us so, on- ly

THE WOMAN'S DEAD

Music by JOHN KANDER
Lyrics by FRED EBB
Additional Lyrics by
RUPERT HOLMES and JOHN KANDER

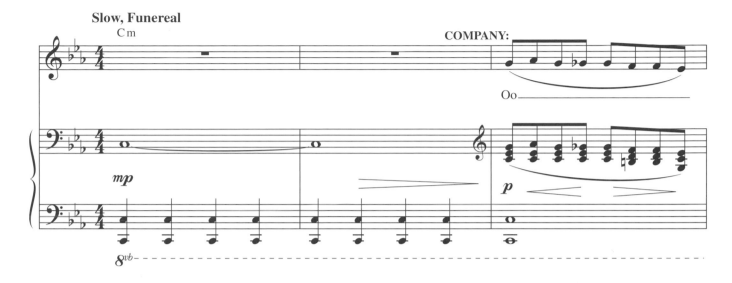

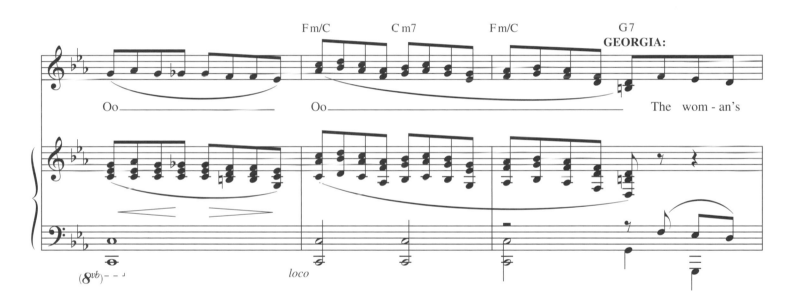

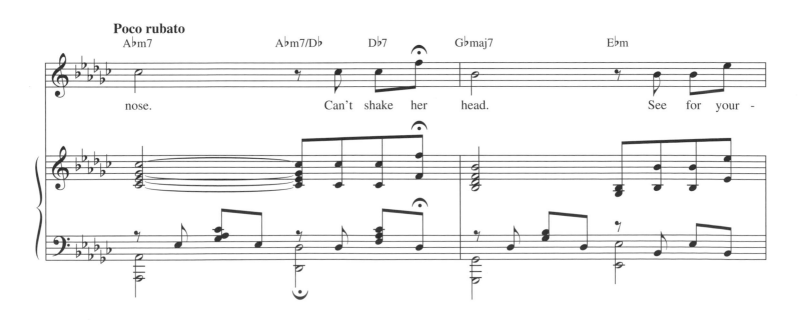

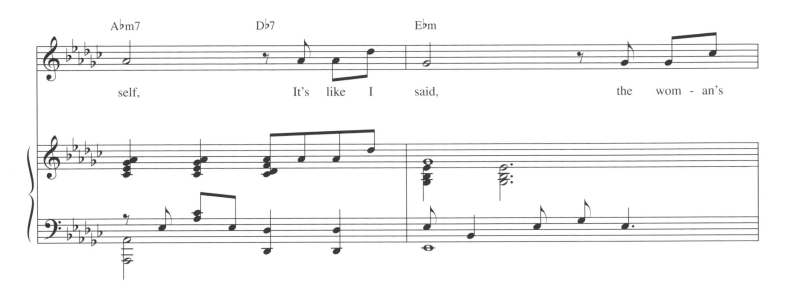

self, It's like I said, the wom-an's

def - i - nite - ly,___ pos - i - tive - ly,

(CIOFFI enters)

molto rall.

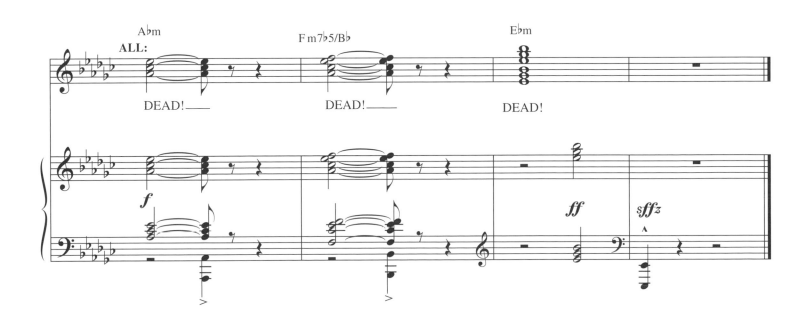

ALL:

DEAD!___ DEAD!___ DEAD!

SHOW PEOPLE

Music by JOHN KANDER
Lyrics by FRED EBB
Additional Lyrics by RUPERT HOLMES

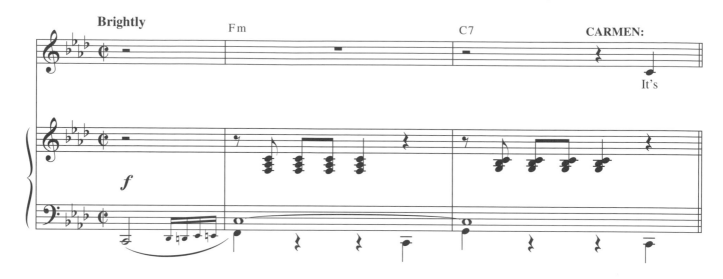

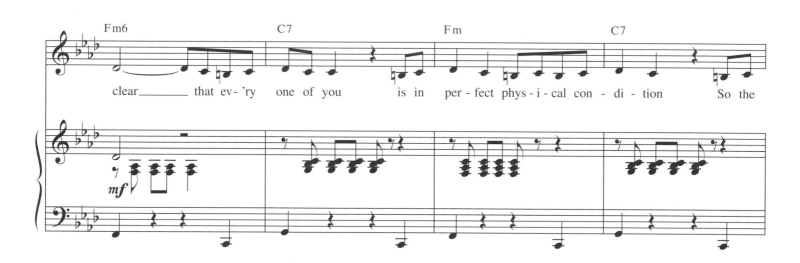

Gm   Gm7   A7   Dm

au - di - ence paid plen - ty to sit there and clap.____

G 13   Gm7   C7

Hear - ing you sing,____ watch - ing you tap.____

Did you

A little brighter

F   Fmaj9   C9sus

know your den - tist longs to be in show bus' - ness? Your

Fmaj9

win - dow wash - er wants to be a star.

Eb/F

F9

And though your

Bbmaj7   Bbm6

an - a - lyst may_____ nev - er couch it that way_____

Am7   Am7/D

Am7   D9   Gm7   C13   F

You don't know how luck - y you are!

CIOFFI:

Some po -

poco rit.

CARMEN, CIOFFI:

Ask your clean-ing la-dy, "Don't you dream of show bus'-ness? To vo-cal-ize____ or stretch be-side a barre?"_____ Her af- firm-a-tive shrug____ as she sham-poos your rug____ Lets you

feel that spot - light hit me and I'm gone!_____ At the

Tempo I°

last cur - tain call_____ I'm the en - vy of all,_____ So I

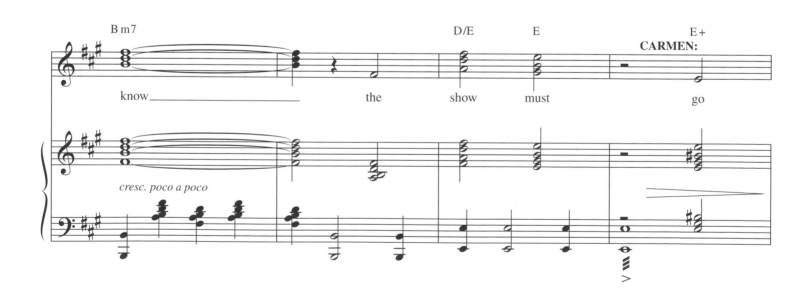

know_____ the show must go

COFFEE SHOP NIGHTS

Music and Lyrics by
JOHN KANDER

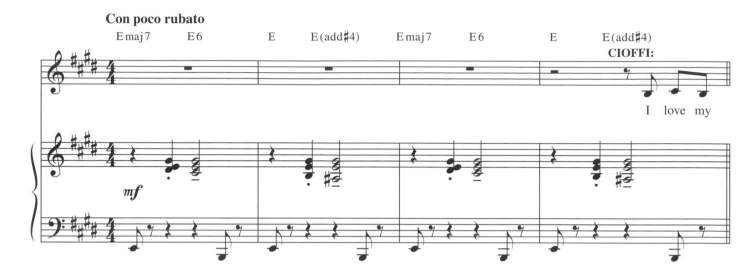

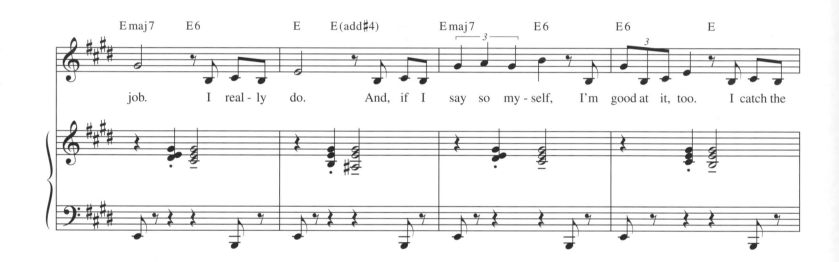

good life! Not ex - act - ly sub - lime.

When I've

Con poco moto

fin - ished my work, And I crawl in - to bed, I re - flect, as I turn out the

mp richly

lights,_____ That the day that's to come And the

week that's a - head Will be lunch count - er morn - ings_____ And

44

I MISS THE MUSIC

Music and Lyrics by
JOHN KANDER

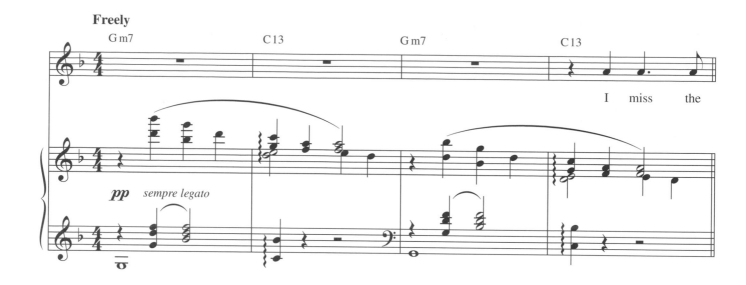

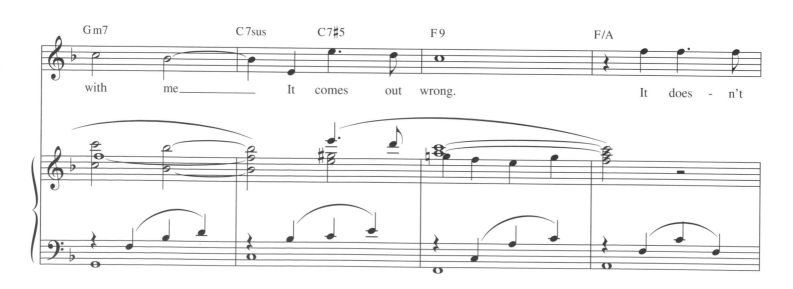

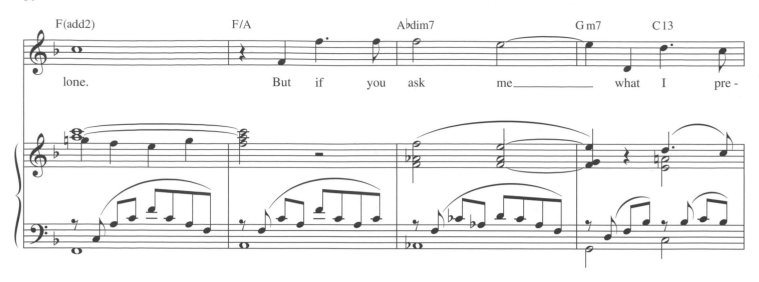

A 9sus F♯m/A A 9sus F♯m/A
No one tells you, "That's not fun-ny." No one says, "Let's cut that bar."
F♯m B 7 E m7(add4)
No one makes you bet - ter than you are.
poco accel.
Con poco moto
F♯maj7/C♯ G♯m9 G♯m7 C♯7♭9
I can't pre -
f
dim. poco a poco
F♯(add2) F♯ F♯maj7/A♯ F♯/A♯ G♯m7 C♯9sus C♯7♯5
tend. I miss the mu - sic. I miss my

THATAWAY!

Music by JOHN KANDER
Lyrics by JOHN KANDER and RUPERT HOLMES

Poco rubato, con moto

GEORGIA:

He made a

get - a - way.   He left me   flat - a - way.   At times like

this,   a mod - ern   miss should   gal - lop   that - a - way.   When love goes

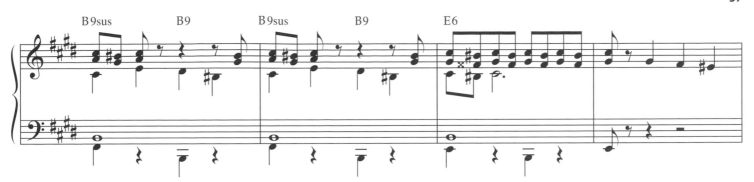

If he's in

Par - a - guay   or e - ven Man - de - lay,   I'll grab my

A little slower - conversationally

HE DID IT

Music by JOHN KANDER
Lyrics by FRED EBB
Additional Lyrics by RUPERT HOLMES

(cue) **CHARACTER 1:**
If I had to bet, I'd say he did it.

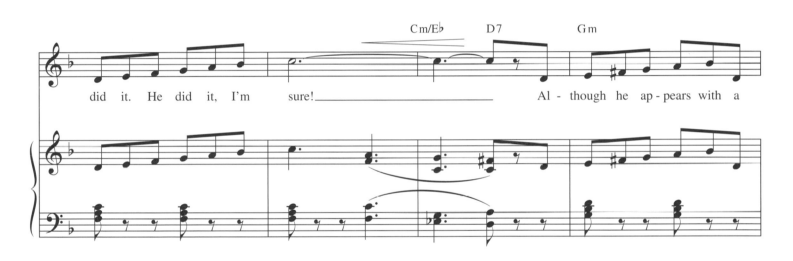

IT'S A BUSINESS

Music by JOHN KANDER
Lyrics by FRED EBB

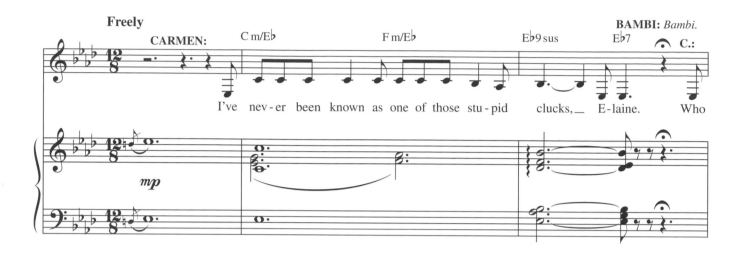

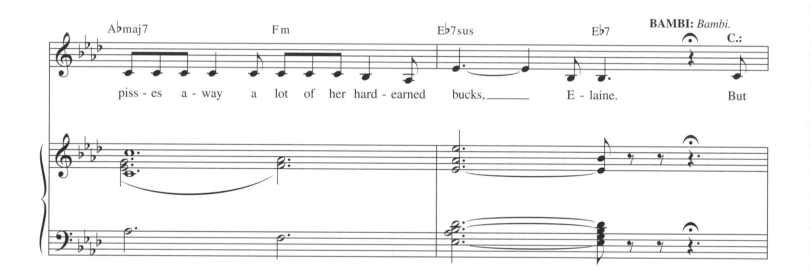

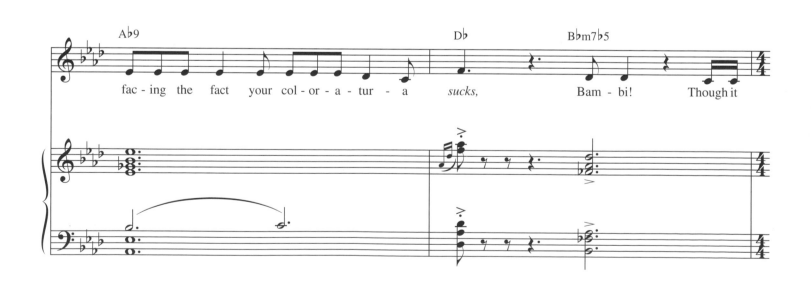

Con moto

breaks your moth-er's heart, For-get a-bout the part. It's time for you to know why I

real - ly backed this show.

A Tempo - Coarse Strut

You

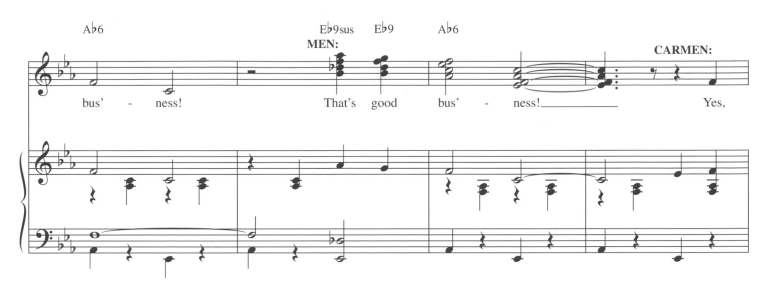

KANSASLAND

Music by JOHN KANDER
Lyrics by JOHN KANDER and RUPERT HOLMES

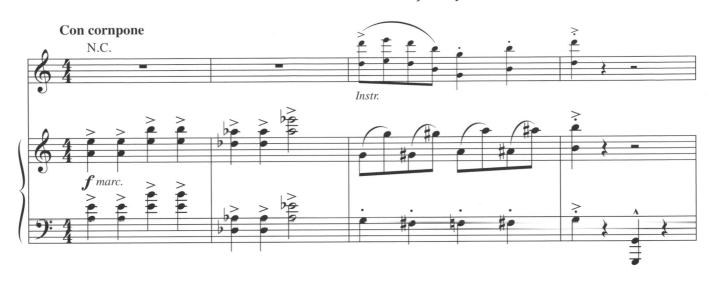

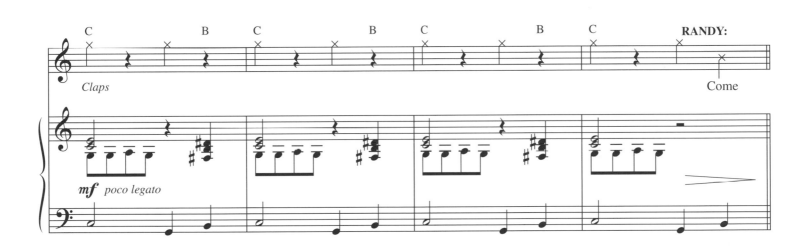

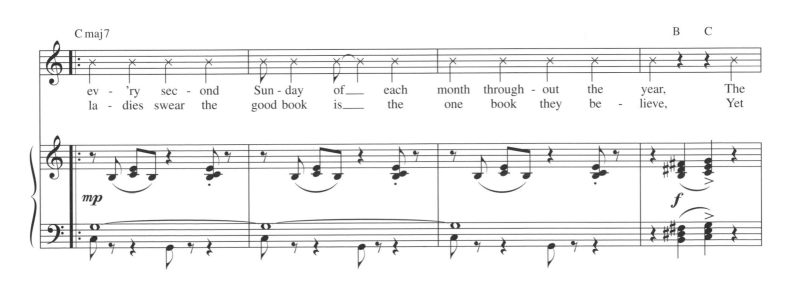

Kan - sas - land ain't no fin - er place to live and die than

Kan - sas - land where your home is on the range, but in

Kan - sas - land it ain't too smart to be too

strange.

A TOUGH ACT TO FOLLOW

Music by JOHN KANDER
Lyrics by FRED EBB

Moderately

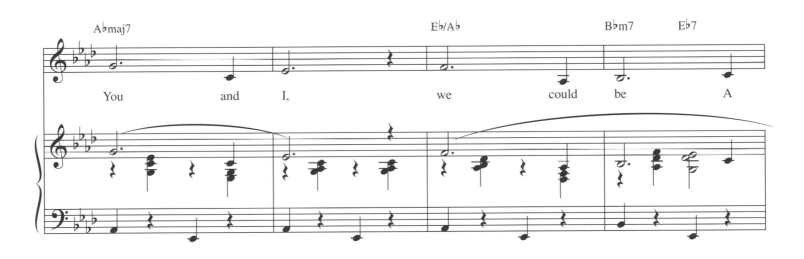

You and I, we could be A

tough act to fol-low. Can't you see?

IN THE SAME BOAT

Music by JOHN KANDER
Lyrics by FRED EBB

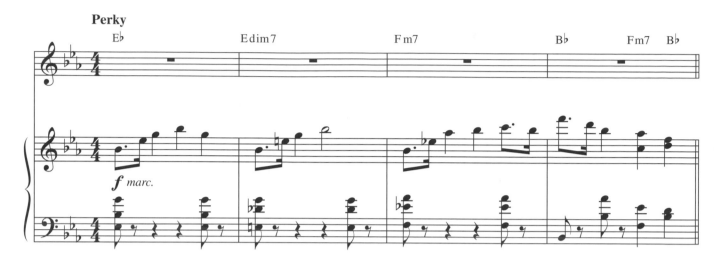

In the same boat, On the same sea, Shak-in' in-side as the tide keeps ris-in'.

Nar-y a ship, Nar-y a sail, Nar-y a soul on the whole ho-ri-zon.

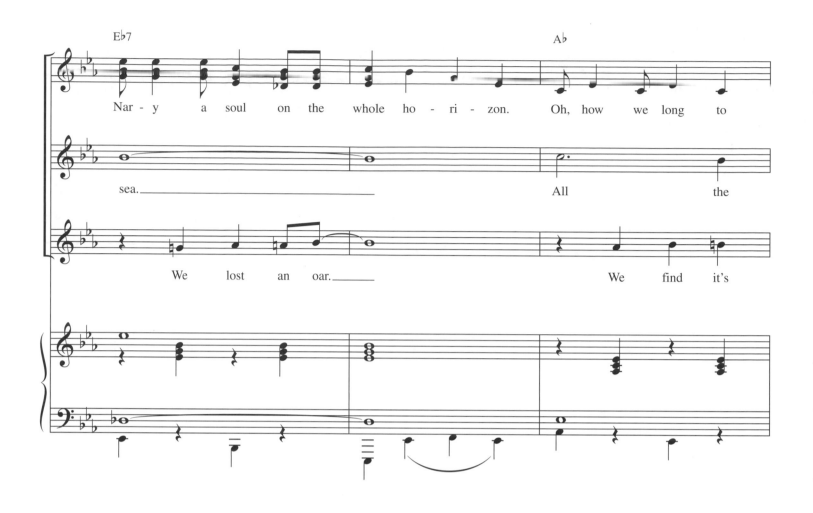

Nar - y a soul on the whole ho - ri - zon. Oh, how we long to

sea._____ All the

We lost an oar._____ We find it's

stand still. Stom - achs are in dis - tress._____

planks are spring - ing a leak. We'd

all we can do___ To calm the craft.___ Fur - ther - more, lit - tle chum,__

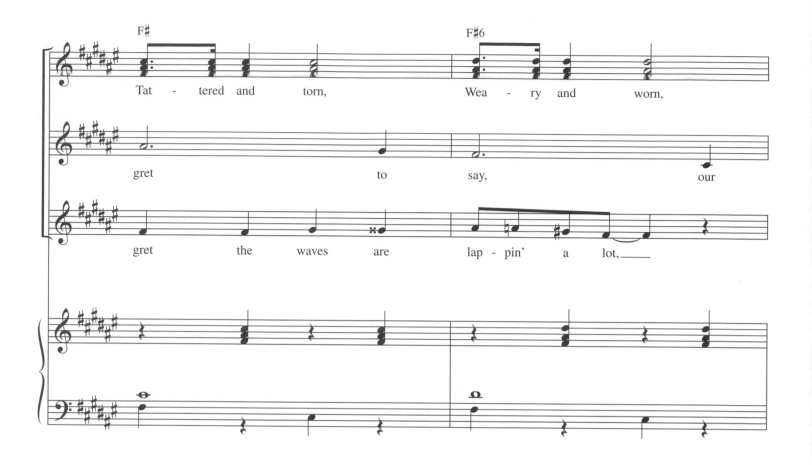

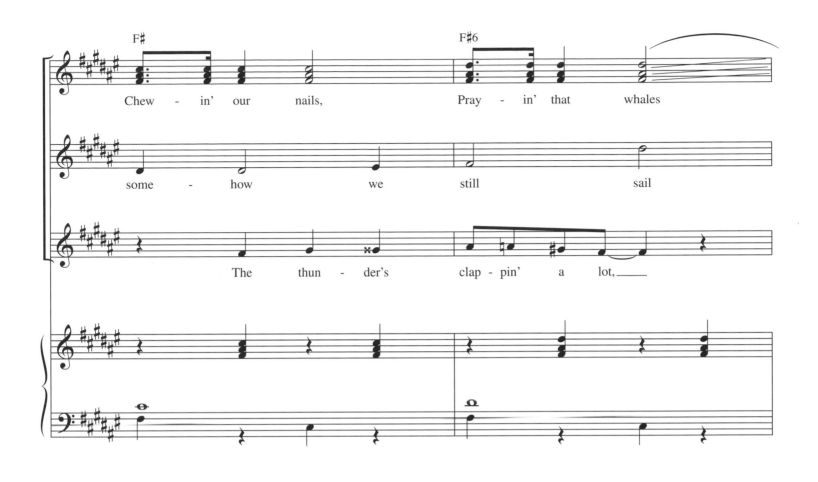